DENISE LEVERTOV

COLLECTED
EARLIER
POEMS
1940~1960

Books by Denise Levertov

DENISE LEVERTOV

COLLECTED
EARLIER
POEMS
1940~1960

A NEW DIRECTIONS BOOK

Grateful acknowledgment is made to the editors and publishers of magazines and anthologies in which some of the poems in this collection originally appeared: *Ark II Moby I, Black Mountain Review, Canadian Poetry Magazine, Combustion, Contact, Evergreen Review, The Fifties, Gangrel, Jargon, Mademoiselle, The Nation, The New Berkeley Review, New British Poets, New Directions in Prose and Poetry, A New Folder, New York Portfolio, Noonday Review, Origin, Partisan Review, Poems from the Floating World, Poetry, Poetry Quarterly, The Texas Quarterly, Verse, Voices.*

Manufactured in the United States of America
First published clothbound and as New Directions Paperback 475 in 1979
Published simultaneously in Canada by George J. McLeod Ltd., Toronto

Library of Congress Cataloging in Publication Data

Levertov, Denise, 1923–
    Collected earlier poems, 1940–1960.
    (A New Directions Book)
    Includes index.
PS3562.E88A17   1979   811'.5'4   78-26199
ISBN 0–8112–0717–x
ISBN 0–8112–0718–8 pbk.

New Directions Books are published for James Laughlin by New Directions Publishing Corporation, 80 Eighth Avenue, New York 10011

Contents

I began writing at five years old, but have lost the poems that precede my first *published* poem, "Listening to Distant Guns," written during or just before Dunkirk. In Buckinghamshire, where I was "evacuated," one could hear the big guns across the Channel even though Bucks is an inland county. I have also lost many of the poems written between that one and those included in my first book, *The Double Image,* which was published in 1946 by The Cresset Press. The earliest poems in *The Double Image* were written when I was eighteen or nineteen, and the latest in 1945 (a full year having passed between acceptance and publication).

Of the poems included in the "Early and Uncollected" section of this present collection, some, as will be seen, were composed in England and Europe before I arrived in the United States at the end of 1948, while a few belong to my life in New York City in the 1950's. This whole group is not arranged in strict chronological order, though I have noted the year of composition and, when recalled, the place. Only the last in the group postdates my first U.S. books. *Here and Now* and *Overland to the Islands.*

I would like to mention here my curious publishing history and some kindnesses that helped me along my way long ago: When I was twelve I had the temerity to send some poems to T. S. Eliot, even though I had not shown most of them even to my sister, and certainly to no one else. Months later, when I had forgotten all about this impulsive act, a two- or even three-page typewritten letter from him arrived, full of excellent advice. (Alas, the letter, treasured for many years, vanished in some move from one apartment to another in the 1950's; I've never ceased to hope it may one day resurface . . .) When I was sixteen I became acquainted with Herbert (later Sir Herbert) Read, as I have elsewhere recounted. From him also I received the most kindly encouragement. When I was nineteen I met Charles Wrey Gardiner, and he began to publish me in his magazine, *Poetry Quarterly* (the same that had printed "Listening to Distant Guns," though he had not then been the editor). This led to publication in other little magazines, such as *Outposts* and *Voices*. The editor of one of these—either Denys Val Baker or Howard Sergeant, I'm afraid I can no longer remember which it was—suggested that I take a book-length manuscript to a friend of his at Sylvan Press. Excited, I did so; but Sylvan Press was about to go out of business. The day I picked up my manuscript from them, as requested (I was too naïve to have sent a stamped addressed envelope with it!) I had just succeeded in landing a nursing job I wanted, at St. Luke's Hospital, Fitzroy Square; and so, carried on the wave of my satisfaction about that, I walked into the offices of The Cresset Press, which I caught sight of at the corner of the square upon completing my successful interview with the matron of St. Luke's. Accidentally, I entered by way of the stockroom, and a packer there let me ascend to Irene Calverley's office. She was courteously but firmly instructing me that this was not the way to approach a publisher when something—my youthful appearance (I was twenty-one but looked seventeen) or crestfallen expression—made her decide to look into my ill-typed manuscript anyway. She then told me to leave the package and my address and phone number with her. A few days later she called to say John Hayward had read the poems and accepted them for publication. I remember going into a church somewhere in Soho to kneel in awe because my destiny, which I had always known as a certain but vague form on the far horizon, was beginning to *happen*.

The Double Image came out in 1946, and as previously noted I came to the United States in 1948. I took no steps towards publication of another book, but Kenneth Rexroth included my poems in his anthology *New British Poets* (1949) and friendship with Robert Creeley led to publication in *Origin* and in the *Black Mountain Review*. In the mid '50's (when I was living in New York City) I received a letter from Weldon Kees, who was only a name to me, saying that he'd read and liked my work and wanted to publish a book of it in a small press series he and a printer friend were planning. I was delighted, and sent him a manuscript, with which he was pleased. But before the book went into production came news of his death, or at least of his presumed death by a leap from the Golden Gate Bridge. I never met him. Perhaps a year later, one "Larry Ferling," as Lawrence Ferlinghetti then called himself, wrote to say that my poems had come into his hands after Weldon Kees' death and that he would like to publish them; he was just starting the City Lights Series then.

Not much later Jonathan Williams wrote to say he would like to do a book. Because the Kees/Ferlinghetti offer had come first, I offered Ferlinghetti first choice of all the poems I had by then accumulated (a somewhat larger group than the original Kees project) and gave Jonathan the "rejects" plus what still newer work I had done in the intervening months. Thus, poems that should really have been in a single book together because of their interrelationships were arbitrarily divided between *Here and Now* and *Overland to the Islands*. Robert Duncan, who had read them all in typescript, pointed out to me that I should not have let either book be so loosely, thoughtlessly thrown together; and for the first time I realized that a book of separate poems can in itself be a composition, and that to *compose* a book is preferable to randomly gathering one.

Of all these kindnesses none exceeds, in effect or duration, that of Kenneth Rexroth. He "discovered" me before I came to the United States, and continued to "promote" me after I came here. Probably it was he who showed my poems to Kees and then to Ferlinghetti. Most certainly it was he who persistently brought me to James Laughlin's attention, and so—once James Laughlin felt I had a voice of my own—to the happiness and honor of becoming in 1959 a New Directions author. I have actually met Kenneth only a few times in all the years, and after 1948 rarely exchanged letters with him; yet his unswerving concern for my work has undoubtedly benefitted my life and fortune. Publication of this book seems a fitting time to say thanks to him, and to the others I've mentioned.

EARLY AND UNCOLLECTED POEMS

Listening to Distant Guns

The roses tremble; oh, the sunflower's eye
Is opened wide in sad expectancy.
Westward and back the circling swallows fly,
The rooks' battalions dwindle near the hill.

That low pulsation in the east is war:
No bell now breaks the evening's silent dream.
The bloodless clarity of evening's sky
Betrays no whisper of the battle-scream.

1940

Sarnen

Under the harvest sun the heart
ripens on its wall;
under the heat of noon the mind
like a leaf is cool.
The angelus and the goatbell
sway across the grass;
butterflies in blue mid-air
touch and spin apart.
Any attempted dream must fall
to ruin in this light, must pass
before the mocking glance
of idle animals.
There is no need to escape
from the motionless mountain
there is no need to escape
when here the indifferent lake
accepts a nervous image,

demands no affirmation
of innocence or faith.

Switzerland, 1946

Interim

For K. S.

A black page of night
flutters: dream on or waken,
words will spring from darkness now,
gold-bright, to fill the hollow mind
laid still to hear them, as an iron cup
laid on the window-ledge, would fill with rain.
Not more alone
waking than sleeping, in darkness than in light,
yet it is now we can assume
an attitude more listening than longing,
extend invisible antennæ towards
some intimation, echo, emanation
falling slowly like a destined feather
that lights at last before the feet
of hesitating fear. Not less alone
in city than in solitude, at least
this time—an hour or minute?—left between
dreaming and action, where the only glitter
is the soft gleam of words, affording
intimacy with each submerged regret,
awakes a new lucidity in pain,
so that with day we meet
familiar angels that were lately tears
and smile to know them only fears transformed.

London, 1946

4

Footprint of fury quiet, now, on the salt sand
hills couched like hares in blue grass of the air
water lifting its glass to star and candle
time curled at rest in a ready hand.

No claw of wind plucking the strings of the sea
never a bough bent, no sad fruit falling;
never a rage of autumn's angry angel
but sails in to the haven of a tree.

O fear dissolves here and now I cease
to hear the hammer the axe the bone the bell,
shade of a shade grown still, grief of a grief
lulled in green hollows of a well of peace.

1946

The Anteroom

Out of this anteroom whose light is broken
by slatted blinds and rustling portières,
a tentative room too near the street,
pierced with street voices and the sound of horns,
uneasy halting place of travelling ghosts:

out of this season of uprooted hours,
where time, that should grow round as hanging fruit,
rushes like showers of dry and shrivelled leaves,
and no hour quickens into truth; where love,
confused, can never touch or penetrate
a growing dream, but hovers at its side:

Florence, 1948

that love, that dream, must travel
into wide landscapes where the heart has rest,
and quietly (as stones, pure on the still earth,
await a strange completion into dream,
by the slow rain, or by a man's desire)
await their transformation into life.

Folding a Shirt

For S.P.

Folding a shirt, a woman stands
still for a moment, to recall
warmth of flesh; her careful hands

heavy on a sleeve, recall
a gesture, or the touch of love;
she leans against the kitchen wall,

listening for a word of love,
but only finds a sound like fear
running through the rooms above.

With folded clothes she folds her fear,
but cannot put desire away,
and cannot make the silence hear.

Unwillingly she puts away
the bread, the wine, the knife,
smooths the bed where lovers lay,

while time's unhesitating knife
cuts away the living hours,
the common rituals of life.

London, 1946

Some are too much at home in the role of wanderer,
watcher, listener; who, by lamplit doors
that open only to another's knock,
commune with shadows and are happier
with ghosts than living guests in a warm house.
They drift about the darkening city squares,
coats blown in evening winds and fingers feeling
familiar holes in pockets, thinking: Life
has always been a counterfeit, a dream
where dreaming figures danced behind the glass.
Yet as they work, or absently stand at a window
letting a tap run and the plates lie wet,
while the bright rain softly shines upon slates,
they feel the whole of life is theirs, the music,
"colour, and warmth, and light"; hands held
safe in the hands of love; and trees beside them
dark and gentle, growing as they grow,
a part of the world with fire and house and child.
The undertone of all their solitude
is the unceasing question, "Who am I?
A shadow's image on the rainy pavement,
walking in wonder past the vivid windows,
a half-contented guest among my ghosts?
Or one who, imagining light, air, sun,
can now take root in life, inherit love?"

London, 1946

The blind tap their way from stone to stone
feel from shadow to shadow, suncaressed
between the plane-trees.
I listen with closed eyes to the dry
autumnal sound of their searching.
Whom the tree grows in, whom clouds compel,
green enters, red, blue of a bell
of a ringing sky; whom wings delight
or waving weed on frayed sleeves of the sea,
I fear the blind: they cannot share my world
but stop its spinning with their heavy shadows.

Paris, 1947

'So You, too . . .'

So you, too, are a part of me. My solitude
always beginning, as grass grows, is a tide
running at daybreak out of the grayrose east
to slide over the sand, encircle
the drowned beauty, the dead bird, the old boot;
my life explores the caves, pours into pools,
hunts with the starry hunters. I stretch out
fingers of grass, fingers of flame, and touch
my own name engraved on air, own flesh
walking towards me down a dream. I wheel
as a wave pounces, unmask the stranger:
you too a part of me, I enter the gate of your eyes,
my beggar, my brother, answer of the sea.

Holland, 1947

Solace

For N.P.

Memories at best are old wives' ghosts,
    transparent and incredible, their chains
    clanking grotesquely. Only an unforeseen
    access of longing in the blood can bear
    the risen burden of true ghosts, that are
    powerful and near as, on a moor,
    the immanent spirit of a rock may seem; are warm
    to touch, and, fading, undermine
    the elaborate bulwarks of indifference.

Better to drift, happy, among stone faces
    which, looking back, are alive, but exact nothing,
    neither a past nor a future; to commune
    with Apollo's impersonal smile, which surrounds
    your listening silence like a phrase of music.

The head of Euripides or a tense
    Egyptian cat (so still, you feel
    it turns and stretches when you look away)
    are not more distant than a lover
    in a far country (*does it rain there,*
    the small rain in the streets of home?
    Do you sleep sound or hear the dripping eaves?)

Not less real, the melancholy, eager,
    black-olive eyes of lost Byzantium
    than recollected glances met
    last year or yesterday, and now forgotten
    even while longing strives to raise a ghost.

Paris, 1947

Too easy: to write of miracles, dreams where the famous give
mysterious utterance to silent truth;
to confuse snow with the stars,
simulate a star's fantastic wisdom.

Easy like the willow to lament,
rant in trampled roads where pools
are red with sorrowful fires, and sullen rain
drips from the willows' ornamental leaves;
or die in words and angrily turn
to pace like ghosts about the walls of war.

But difficult when, innocent and cold,
day, a bird over a hill, flies in
—resolving anguish to a strange perspective,
a scene within a marble; returning
the brilliant shower of coloured dreams to dust,
a smell of fireworks lingering by canals
on autumn evenings—difficult to write
of the real image, real hand, the heart
of day or autumn beating steadily:
to speak of human gestures, clarify
all the context of a simple phrase
—the hour, the shadow, the fire,
the loaf on a bare table.

Hard, under the honest sun, to weigh
a word until it balances with love—
burden of happiness on fearful shoulders;
in the ease of daylight to discover
what measure has its music, and achieve
the unhaunted country of the final poem.

Sicily, 1948

One is already here whose life
bearing like seed its distant death, shall grow
through human pain, human joy, shall know
music and weeping, only because
the strange flower of your thighs
bloomed in my body. From our joy
begins a stranger's history. Who
is this rider in the dark? We lie
in candlelight; the child's quick unseen movements
jerk my belly under your hand. Who,
conceived in joy, in joy,
lies nine months alone in a walled silence?

Who is this rider in the dark,
nine months the body's tyrant,
nine months alone in a walled silence
our minds cannot fathom?
Who is it will come out of the dark,
whose cries demand our mercy, tyrant
no longer, but alone still, in a solitude
memory cannot reach?
Whose lips will suckle at these breasts,
thirsting, unafraid, for life?
Whose eyes will look out of that solitude?

The wise face of the unborn
ancient and innocent
must change to infant ignorance
before we see it, irrevocable third
looking into our lives; the child
must hunger, sleep, cry, gaze, long weeks
before it learns of laughter. Love can never
wish a life no darkness; but may love
be constant in the life our love has made.

New York, 1949

11

Easels: a high & bare room:
some with charcoal, one with a brush,
some with loud pens in the silence,
at work. The woman
in taut repose, intent:

under violent light that pulls
the weight of breasts to answer the long
shadow of thighs,
confronts angles with receding
planes, makes play with elements.

That they work, that she will not move too soon,
opposes (as Bartok's plucked strings oppose)
the grinding, grinding, grinding of lives,
pounding constant traffic.

On paper, on canvas, stroke, stroke: a counterpoint:
an energy opposing
the squandered energy.

New York, early '50's

A Woman

For L.B.

Exciting not by excitement only; subtler:
'beautiful & unhappy' 's not enough:
a woman engrossed
in delight or anguish or simply in passing
from point to point: stretched proudly
ready to twang or sing at pluck or stroke.
Northward: now her green eyes

are looking, looking for a door
to open in a wall where
there's no door, none unless she make it:
an ice-wall to be broken by hand. Northward
in fact and in fact:
now her green eyes
spend their sea-depth & glitter
remotely; she's gone, who stays so strangely.
And we—we look at each other:
'Where should this music be?'

New York, early '50's

An Innocent (II)

(1st version)

At 9 on Hudson St., by 10
   through rotten mounds of foodscraps
in Chelsea, and on, north, with
perhaps some glove (or what?) to show for his pains.

Pink face, curved nose, white mustache,
white hair curling
over his collar; an army greatcoat. A blue sack
      or sometimes a white sack stencilled
      with faded dollar-signs.

It's not his thoroughness and speed
distinguish him so much as the invention
he wears, intimate as a hearing aid: an aid
   to delicate poking:
   a hook
   attached to his arm, projecting
   beyond the hand.

13

One, hearing of
this prince of scavengers, cried out
     in horror at that bad dream of a hook
      (methodical defilement coyly reduced)
and I too recoiled then; but later

thought my disgust false:
for I'd seen on the old man's face
only the calm intense look of a craftsman:
innocent!

He accepts what we reject, endlessly stuffing
his floursack, silent
    (no one speaks to him)
    from can to can—an endless
city of refuse. And makes
some kind of life from it. His face
                  rebukes us.

New York, mid '50's

An Innocent (II)

(2nd version)

Pink faced, white haired, aquiline old man
endlessly stuffing your floursack—with what?
—Scraps from an endless
city of refuse—
        Silent, all day from can to can
picking garbage with an ingenious hook—

It's the hook we most recoil from—
in false disgust—
       Calm, intense—
        the face of a craftsman—innocent!

New York, mid '50's

14

The Whisper

Among the leaves & bell-flowers
he who carved them contrived to
entwine the letters of his name. Other
letters complete the
span of the small round table,
                            but these

don't seem to spell even
in Hungarian. They are probably
            not a code, not
            initials of a phrase, only
            part of a pattern.
                            Yet: it is

a message—some continuing whisper,
            the act of choice of Anders
Szoltesz, alive or dead, drawn to
just these from all the alphabet, to enhance
the table I love for its
solid stance and
involved, angular, delicate ornament.

New York, mid '50's

Today's Saint

O.K., so he's crazy,
            dowser, cloudbuster. But it's his goodness
makes him attempt so variously,
assuming rapports.
                            He's looking
not at the fragments but for

the interplay. It's your pain,
      my grimace, torments him: '
                              why, why
                  the jagged lives.
He wanted, even in his first mistakes
      (the cold girl taken too often
      hating him at last, escaping)
that all should flower, everyone
joyful. If his imagination
proliferates, it is for you. If not,
he gave us the sudden rain last Sunday,
      the darkening. Maybe raindrops?
                  It's a
'means of grace' he's trying to
secure for us.
            'The cloud
compact of energy.' That we may
live.

New York, late '50's

15th Street

Almost dark, and the wind off the river.
It's November. But quite a few
(kids mostly) out on the stoops. A bunch of young girls
posed on the steps of this one,
ladies of the court. Oh, one's the queen,
red hair, & that turn
of the head, a long neck.
A woman in black's going up between them now
slowly, bringing home groceries. 'Where's Johnnie tonight?'
      'Oh, I'm mad at him.'—Deirdre, tossing her head.
'Hah,'—the woman, over her shoulder, in fond contempt,
going on in.

16

The sky has cleared itself of clouds
at always at this hour, preparing
for the stars it's hard to see.
Hockey players on roller skates are
shouting, hard, they glide subtly
to dodge a cab, not looking at it.
Here, a few doors down, two youths reveal & exchange
scraps of their work-world, still new.
'He pushes himself right to the front, this guy,
swearin' and hollerin'. So we said to him, "Listen, mister
there's other people waitin' besides you." '
We. It's here, here, here, 'it frees, it
creates relief.' Poetry, element, in which we move
as fish in water.

         The river-hooting, illusion of north-lights
shaking in fever over 14th, & away uptown, 42nd.
It's getting late, the kids drift off
indoors. Better get supper. Deirdre will forgive
Johnny, later, in this unlit doorway (launderette)
saying 'Goodnight. So long. Goodnight.
            I'll see you around.'

New York, late '50's

Down Here and up There

Swing of the scythe
illuminated, displaced
into my book of hours, the falling
grass, goldleafed
on the uneven
left upper windowpane—

But way up on the hill
the drift of field-air around you,
the scythe singing,
and what birds you may hear.

Maine, early '60's

17

from THE DOUBLE IMAGE (1946)

Durgan

For J.M.

At Durgan waves are black as cypresses,
clear as the water of a wishing well,
caressing the stones with smooth palms, looking
into the pools as enigmatic eyes
peer into mirrors, or music echoes
out of a wood the waking dream of day,
blind eyelids lifting to a coloured world.

Now with averted head your living ghost
walks in my mind, your shadow leans
over the half-door of dream; your footprint lies
where gulls alight; shade of a shade, you laugh.
But separate, apart, you are alive:
you have not died, therefore I am alone.

Like birds, cottages white and grey
alert on rocks are gathered, or low
under branches, dark but not desolate;
shells move over sand, or seaweed gleams
with their clear yellow, as tides recede.
Serene in storm or eloquent in sunlight
sombre Durgan where no strangers come
awaits us always, but is always lost:
we are separate, sharing no secrets, each alone;
you will listen no more, now, to the sounding sea.

The Barricades

If now you cannot hear me, it is because
your thoughts are held by sounds of destiny
or turn perhaps to darkness, magnetized,

as a doomed ship upon the Manacles
is drawn to end its wandering and down
into the stillness under rock and wave
to lower its bright figurehead; or else
you never heard me, only listening
to that implicit question in the shade,
duplicity that gnaws the roots of love.

If now I cannot see you, or be sure
you ever stirred beyond the walls of dream,
rising, unbroken battlements, to a sky
heavy with constellations of desire,
it is because those barricades are grown
too tall to scale, too dense to penetrate,
hiding the landscape of your distant life
in which you move, as birds in evening air
far beyond sight trouble the darkening sea
with the low piping of their discontent.

The Dreamers

The sleeping sensual head
    lies nearer than her hand,
but secret and remote,
    an impenetrable land.

Each, in the hardening crystal
    a prisoner of pride,
abstractedly caresses
    the stranger at his side,

duality's abyss
    unspanned by desire,
reason's cold salamander
    scatheless in the fire.

She hears the sound of midnight
    that breaks like a sea,
and leans above the sleeper
    as secretive as he.

Casselden Road, N.W. 10

For Marya

The wind would fan the life-green fires that smouldered
under the lamps, and from the glistening road
draw out deep shades of rain, and we would hear
the beat of rain on darkened panes, the sound
of night and no one stirring but ourselves,
leaning still from the window. No one else
will remember this. No one else will remember.

Shadows of leaves like riders hurried by
upon the wall within. The street would fill
with phantasy, the night become
a river or an ocean where the tree
and silent lamp were sailing; the wind would fail
and sway towards the light. And no one else
will remember this. No one else will remember.

Enter with riches. Let your image wear
brocade of fantasy, and bear your part
with all the actor's art and arrogance.
Your eager bride, the flickering moth that burns
upon your mouth, brings to your dark reserve
a glittering dowry of desire and dreams.

These leaves of lightness and these weighty boughs
that move alive to every living wind,
dews, flowers, fruit, and bitter rind of life,
the savour of the sea, all sentient gifts
you will receive, deserve due ritual;
eloquent, just, and mighty one, adorn
your look at last with sorrow and with fire.
Enter with riches, enviable prince.

Christmas 1944

Bright cards above the fire bring no friends near,
fire cannot keep the cold from seeping in.
Spindrift sparkle and candles on the tree
make brave pretence of light; but look out of doors:
Evening already surrounds the curtained house,
draws near, watches;
gardens are blue with frost, and every carol
bears a burden of exile, a song of slaves.
Come in, then, poverty, and come in, death:
this year too many lie cold, or die in cold
for any small room's warmth to keep you out.
You sit in empty chairs, gleam in unseeing eyes;

24

having no home now, you cast your shadow
over the atlas, and rest in the restlessness
of our long nights as we lie, dreaming of Europe.

A painted bird or boat above the fire,
a fire in the hearth, a candle in the dark,
a dark excited tree, fresh from the forest,
are all that stand between us and the wind.
The wind has tales to tell of sea and city,
a plague on many houses, fear knocking on the doors;
how venom trickles from the open mouth of death,
and trees are white with rage of alien battles.
Who can be happy while the wind recounts
its long sagas of sorrow? Though we are safe
in a flickering circle of winter festival
we dare not laugh; or if we laugh, we lie,
hearing hatred crackle in the coal,
the voice of treason, the voice of love.

Ballad

Bravely in a land of dust
we set out, as pilgrims must,
you, who fear the dark, and I
fearing winter in the sky.

Dark and cold the winter cloud
hung above the hill of lies
and my phoenix cried aloud,
took flight toward the eastern skies.

Do you think I shall forget
the tried intent, the diamond set

solitary and forlorn
in a coronet of thorn?

Beyond the high and frozen hill
beyond the forest black and still
I shall find you, where the fire
burns the wings of my desire.

Midnight Quatrains

I love to see, in golden matchlight,
intimate contours of a face
like discovered innocence
in dusty annals of disgrace.

Caught in a minute's spell of love,
a microcosm of sudden flame,
I learn this new geography—
wilderness I could never tame.

Listening to rain around the corner
we sense a dream's reality,
and know, before the match goes out,
ephemeral eternity.

HERE AND NOW (1957)

The Gypsy's Window

It seems a stage
backed by imaginations of velvet,
cotton, satin, loops and stripes—

A lovely unconcern
scattered the trivial plates, the rosaries
and centered
a narrownecked dark vase,
unopened yellow and pink
paper roses, a luxury of open red
paper roses—

Watching the trucks go by, from stiff chairs
behind the window show, an old
bandanna'd brutal dignified
woman, a young beautiful woman
her mouth a huge contemptuous rose—

The courage
of natural rhetoric tosses to dusty
Hudson St. the chance of poetry, a chance
poetry gives passion to the roses,
the roses in the gypsy's window in a blue
vase, look real, as unreal
as real roses.

Beyond the End

In 'nature' there's no choice—
     flowers
swing their heads in the wind, sun & moon

are as they are. But we seem
almost to have it (not just
        available death)

It's energy; a spider's thread: not to
'go on living' but to quicken, to activate: extend:
        Some have it, they force it—
with work or laughter or even
        the act of buying, if that's
all they can lay hands on—

                the girls crowding the stores, where light,
                        colour, solid dreams are—what gay
                    desire! It's their festival,
                        ring game, wassail, mystery.

It has no grace like that of
the grass, the humble rhythms, the
falling & rising of leaf and star;
it's barely
a constant. Like salt:
take it or leave it

The 'hewers of wood' & so on; every damn
craftsman has it while he's working
        but it's not
a question of work: some
shine with it, in repose. Maybe it is
response, the will to respond—('reason
can give nothing at all / like
the response to desire') maybe
a gritting of the teeth, to go
just that much further, beyond the end
beyond whatever ends: to begin, to be, to defy.

The Innocent

The cat has his sport
and the mouse suffers
but the cat
     is innocent
  having no image of pain in him

    an angel
    dancing with his prey

carries it, frees it, leaps again
with joy upon his darling plaything

     a dance, a prayer!
  How cruel the cat is to our guilty eyes

The Earthwoman and the Waterwoman

    The earthwoman by her oven
        tends her cakes of good grain.
The waterwoman's children
are spindle thin.
             The earthwoman
     has oaktree arms. Her children
full of blood and milk
    stamp through the woods shouting.
    The waterwoman
sings gay songs in a sad voice
     with her moonshine children.
When the earthwoman
has had her fill of the good day

she curls to sleep in her warm hut
a dark fruitcake sleep
but the waterwoman
        goes dancing in the misty lit-up town
in dragonfly dresses and blue shoes.

The Rights

I want to give you
something I've made

some words on a page—as if
to say 'Here are some blue beads'

or, 'Here's a bright red leaf I found on
the sidewalk' (because

to find is to choose, and choice
is made).   But it's difficult:

so far I've found
nothing but the wish to give. Or

copies of old words? Cheap
and cruel; also senseless:
                        Take

this instead, perhaps—a half-
promise: If

I ever write
a poem of a certain temper

(willful, tender, evasive,
sad & rakish)

I'll give it to you.

People at Night

(*derived from Rilke*)

A night that cuts between you and you
and you   and you   and you
and me : jostles us apart, a man elbowing
through a crowd.   We won't
                look for each other, either—
wander off, each alone, not looking
in the slow crowd. Among sideshows
                under movie signs,
                pictures made of a million lights,
                giants that move and again move
                again, above a cloud of thick smells,
                franks, roasted nutmeats—

Or going up to some apartment, yours
                            or yours, finding
someone sitting in the dark:
who is it, really? So you switch the
light on to see: you know the name but
who is it?
        But you won't see.

The fluorescent light flickers sullenly, a
pause. But you command. It grabs

33

each face and holds it up
by the hair for you, mask after mask.
     You   and you   and you   and I repeat
        gestures that make do when speech
        has failed   and talk
        and talk, laughing, saying
        'I', and 'I',
meaning 'Anybody.'
             No one.

The Flight*

     'The will is given us that
        we may know the
delights of surrender.' Blake with
tense mouth, crouched small (great forehead,
somber eye) amid a crowd's tallness in a narrow room.
            The same night
a bird caught in my room, battered
from wall to wall, missing the window over & over
                  (till it gave up and
                     huddled half-dead on a shelf, and I
                     put up the sash against the cold)

and waking at dawn I again
pushed the window violently down, open
             and the bird gathered itself and flew
             straight out
             quick and calm (over the radiant chimneys—

* The quoted words were spoken by Blake in my dream. This was
London, 1945.—D.L.

Maybe I'm a 'sick part of a
sick thing'
　　　　maybe something
　　has caught up with me
certainly there is a
mist between us
　　　　　　I can barely
see you
　　but your hands
are two animals that push the
mist aside and touch me.

Among its petals the rose
still holds
　　　　a few tears of the morning rain that
broke it from its stem.
　　　　　　In each
shines a speck of
　　　　　　red light, darker even
than the rose. Phoenix-tailed
slateblue martins pursue
　　one　　another, spaced out
in hopeless hope, circling
　　the porous clay vase, dark from
the water in it. Silence
surrounds the facts. A language
still unspoken.

35

To sit and sit like the cat
and think my thoughts through—
that might be a deep pleasure:

to learn what news
persistence might discover,
and like a woman knitting

make something from the
skein unwinding, unwinding,
something I could wear

or something you could wear
when at length I rose to meet you
outside the quiet sitting-room

(the room of thinking and knitting
the room of cats and women)
among the clamor of

cars and people,
the stars drumming and poems
leaping from shattered windows.

Le Bateleur

'Why should a legerdemainist be placed at the head of this marvelous game? Was it to indicate that despite every effort to read order into the world one remains the victim of illusion?'

The Mirror of Magic

The bank teller has
a constant chance to play such
lovely games, flickering
so much money in such
brilliant fingers, the
clean nails glinting and
the bills forming myriad
patterns like a
magician's Japanese fan, then
coming to rest in little
neat blocks, secured by
rubber-bands, with which
one might build
makebelieve houses; and
always there is
more and more money for his
virtuoso hands to
exercise their trivial powers on,
as water
in the great fountains never
gives out, even
in times of drought, because
they don't waste it—the
same water goes
down and through the
pipes after
its supreme moment of
release—always back again, with
civic prudence.

Don't forget the crablike
hands, slithering
among the keys.
Eyes shut, the downstream
play of sound lifts away from
the present, drifts you
off your feet : too easily let off.

So look: that almost painful
movement restores the pull, incites
the head with the heart : a tension, as of
actors at rehearsal, who move
this way, that way, on a bare stage, testing
their diagonals, in common clothes.

Jackson Square

Bravo! the brave sunshine.
A triangle of green green contains
the sleek and various pigeons
the starving inventors and all
who sit on benches in the morning,
to sun tenacious hopes—indeed
a gay morning for hope to feed on
greedy as the green
and gray
and purple-preening birds
feeding in a flock, now here, now there,
parading for the pleasure of old heroes
and witches, all, all the forlorn.

38

black black on white white
not vague darkness
black defined, black concentrate
crystal-pointed white

rigging, a line of land
nails, wires
lines alive, acts of language
constellations of black

counter to 'unlived life' (passing
repassing, drooping,
senselessly reviving)

energy, gay, terrible, rare,
a hope, man-made.

Xmas Trees on the Bank's Façade

In wind & cold sun the small lights
wink rapidly, pale
                    (excited) among
agitated green, the needle fringes of two
high trees. Wiring looped from branch to branch.
Babies, pushed by, look up, are reluctant
to pass, stretch back their arms.
    The tellers survey from their cages
    the silent swinging of gold-edged doors.
    Money come, money go.

Don't go in. Look: whether the wind,
or lights in daylight, or the
cut trees' lifelike movement, there's
something wild and

                    (beyond clerks & clients)
joyful here. Answerable to no one; least to us.

                                  An idiot joy, to recall
the phoenix joys that mock dead fires
  and whisk
        the ashes with their wings.

Zest

DISPOSE YOUR ENERGIES
PRACTISE ECONOMIES
GO INDOORS, REFUSING
TO ATTEND THE EVENING LANGUORS OF SPRING

WORK BY A STRONG LIGHT
SCOUR THE POTS
DESTROY OLD LETTERS

FINALLY BEFORE SLEEP
WALK ON THE ROOF WHERE
THE SMELL OF SOOT RECALLS A
SNOWFALL.
        UP
OVER THE RED DARKNESS DOLPHINS
ROLL, ROLL, AND TUMBLE, FLASHING THE
SPRAY OF A GREEN SKY.

Below the
   darkening fading
rose
      (to which, straining
      upward, black
      branches address them-
      selves, clowns of alas)
the lights

in multitudinous
windows
        are
   bells in Java

A sense
of festival
   but
somewhere far-off;
   sounds from
over water

the frosty field un-
dulates from
Holland to Mexico:
        space, or
space as dreams
dissolve it

To lay garlands at your feet
because you stand
dark in the light, or lucent
in the dark air of the mind's world
solitary in your empire of magic,
undiminished

and doors are slammed in your face
and stony faces pass you wideawake
and you sing
dreaming wideawake with stone eyes
undiminished

wreaths of hummingbird color
at your feet
and white, and dark leaves, shadows
of moonlight where you sit in sunlight
near the bright sea, listening

to the crash and sighing, crash
and sighing dance of the words.

Mrs. Cobweb*

Her dress was too tight, she had
fits & starts of violent memory that threw
daily memories down the airshaft, she looked
into the cupboard and found
a bone
        that changed into a shadow
                that stole

* A lady who used to send me her poems in the mid '50's; mad
poems in which here and there a marvellous image gleamed.

some treasure from its hiding place behind
the clock, she could not follow, her dress
clutched her,
              but there were days
when shreds of light, fringes of sun
caught her up & whizzed away with her
along serene trolley lines, she reached
for anything & could keep
whatever she could touch, she made:
              a collage of torn leaves she had touched,
              a glass moon-reflector,
often she almost spoke, sharp stars
got tangled in her hair, dazzled by the quietly
shining tracks she wondered if they had passed
the place of arrival?

Everything that Acts Is Actual

From the tawny light
from the rainy nights
from the imagination finding
itself and more than itself
alone and more than alone
at the bottom of the well where the moon lives,
can you pull me

into December? a lowland
of space, perception of space
towering of shadows of clouds blown upon
clouds over
              new ground, new made
under heavy December footsteps? *the only
way to live?*

The flawed moon
acts on the truth, and makes
an autumn of tentative
silences.
You lived, but somewhere else,
your presence touched others, ring upon ring,
and changed. Did you think
I would not change?

                    The black moon
turns away, its work done. A tenderness,
unspoken autumn.
We are faithful
only to the imagination. *What the
imagination*
        seizes
as beauty must be truth. What holds you
to what you see of me is
that grasp alone.

The Lovers

She: Since you have made me beautiful
     I am afraid
              not to be beautiful.
     The silvery dark mirror
     looks past me: I
     cannot accept its silence
     the silence of your
     absence. I want
     my love for you to
     shine from my eyes and hair
            till all the world wonders
     at the light your love has made.

He: At night, waking alone,
   I see you as if in a clear light
   a flower held in the
   teeth of the dark.
   The mirror caught in its solitude
   cannot believe you as I believe.

The Bird

That crazy bird
always laughing—
he sits on the wall they are building,
the wall
which will hide the horizon,
and laughs like mad every time
we open our mouths to say
I love you I hate you etc.
He came only since
the green rain came and
softened everything, making
mud of the cracked
selfrespecting earth and rotting
the red flowers from their stems. Yes,
the rain, the trucks full
of pink bricks, that crazy
eavesdropping bird, came
together and finished
the days of burning, and silence, and distance.

Who'd believe me if
I said, 'They took and

split me open from
scalp to crotch, and

still I'm alive, and
walk around pleased with

the sun and all
the world's bounty.' Honesty

isn't so simple:
a simple honesty is

nothing but a lie.
Don't the trees

hide the wind between
their leaves and

speak in whispers?
The third dimension

hides itself.
If the roadmen

crack stones, the
stones are stones:

but love
cracked me open

and I'm
alive to

46

tell the tale—but not
honestly:

the words
change it. Let it be—

here in the sweet sun
—a fiction, while I

breathe and
change pace.

The Marriage

You have my
attention: which is
a tenderness, beyond
what I may say. And I have
your constancy to
           something beyond myself.
The force
of your commitment charges us—we live
in the sweep of it, taking courage
one from the other.

The Marriage (II)

I want to speak to you.
To whom else should I speak?

It is you who make
a world to speak of.
In your warmth the
fruits ripen—all the
apples and pears that grow
on the south wall of my
head. If you listen
it rains for them, then
they drink. If you
speak in response
the seeds
jump into the ground.
Speak or be silent: your silence
will speak to me.

Laying the Dust

What a sweet smell rises
        when you lay the dust—
bucket after bucket of water thrown
on the yellow grass.
                        The water
flashes
each time you
make it leap—
        arching its glittering back.
The sound of
                more water
pouring into the pail
almost quenches my thirst.
Surely when flowers
grow here, they'll not
smell sweeter than this
        wet ground, suddenly black.

That ancient rockface, rosecolor,
image of steadfastness,
                              gathers the light
through the day and after sundown
and makes of it
something one cannot
            call light nor color : an artifact,
as if a smile
broke some ravaged face
                              and remained
in the glowing eyes, innocent.

Tomatlan (Variations)

i

The sea quiet, shadow-colored and
without shadows.
From which shall rise
the sea wind, moving
swiftly towards the
steep jungles. The sea wind
the awakener.

ii

The sea wind is
a panther moving
swiftly towards the
mountain jungles.

Its silky fur
brushes me.

iii

The green palmettos of the
blue jungle
shake their
green breasts, their stiff
green hair—
the wind, the sea wind is come
and touches them
lightly, and strokes them, and
screws them, until they
are blue flames,
green smoke, and
screws them again.

iv

At the touch
of the sea wind
        the palms
shake their green breasts, their

        rustling fingers—
flames of desire and pleasure.
The sea wind that

        moves like a panther
blows the spray inland.
           Voluptuous

and simple—the world is
larger than one had thought.
It is a

new peace
shades the mind here
with jungle shadows
     frayed by the
sea wind.

Poem from Manhattan

Green-spined
river-bounded
desired of summer storms

          (city, act of joy

Spring evenings in sea-light
facades relax
steel & stone float among clouds

          (city, act of power

And always nightfall flicks
fantasy on black air
     chips of light
flashing   scattered

          (city, act of energy

Over littered avenues
& yawn of brakes at the lights
     hesitation of dawn
     dazed behind smoke feathers

          (city, act of hope

But down, past many windows
    each holding less,
less light—
        down—
each weak pane tossing, feebly handing, letting drop
    pale suns to lower panes—
        fall
    many fathoms down

            (city, desolation

        fall
to cracks between cages
where men are walking
jostled, in dirty light
(reflected light)
are running

            (city, gesture of greed

the derelict & the diamond-sharp
in shadow of inordinate monuments

It is to them
who speaks must speak
Precise
as rain's first
spitting words on the pavement
        pick out
            the core
        lost impulse

            (give it back

OVERLAND TO THE ISLANDS (1958)

Overland to the Islands

Let's go—much as that dog goes,
intently haphazard. The
Mexican light on a day that
'smells like autumn in Connecticut'
makes iris ripples on his
black gleaming fur—and that too
is as one would desire—a radiance
consorting with the dance.
            Under his feet
rocks and mud, his imagination, sniffing,
engaged in its perceptions—dancing
edgeways, there's nothing
the dog disdains on his way,
nevertheless he
keeps moving, changing
pace and approach but
not direction—'every step an arrival.'

The Palm Tree

The bright moon stranded like a whale
the east yellow
and the mistral furious
out of the back hills seawards in black flames.

How the mule-eared palm, half paralyzed
has quickened overnight! Scraping
leaves beating!
           (strained flags . . .)
The palm tree in frenzy!

At once the mind, agape,
                              scavenging:

What's human here? what hope is here?
thumbing the dry leaves
eager, eager, for the fabulous
poem there may be
in this delight or battle
day coming and the moon not gone.

And all morning the palm tree
thick trunk immobile
                              abandons
its awkward leaves
                    (all its life awake
                    in struggling leaves . . .)
And only after the wind
is quenched
the tree dull
a quietness come
does the scraping mind perceive
                              what is possible:
there are no miracles but facts.
To see! (there might be work
      a challenge, a poem)

The squat palm!

The Way Through

Let the rain plunge radiant
through sulky thunder
rage on rooftops

56

let it scissor and bounce its denials
on concrete slabs and black
roadways. Flood the streets. It's much

but not enough, not yet: persist,
rain, real rain, sensuous,
swift, released from

vague skies, the tedium
up there.

Under scared bucking trees
the beach road washed out—

trying to get by on the verge
is no good, earth crumbles into the
brown waterfall, but he backs up
the old car again and CHARGES.

The water flies in the halfwit's eyes
who didn't move fast enough
'Who do you think I am, a horse?'
but we made it—

Drown us, lose us,
rain, let us loose, so,
to lose ourselves, to career
up the plunge of the hill

A Story, a Play*

Not to take
that which is given, to overlook

* *A Dream of Love* (W.C.W.) and *Jardou* (R.C.)

the grace of it (these fragments
    of lives, broken off for you, or
    you might say drops of quicksilver
    alive, rolling for your eyes' pleasure)

not to take—that's
the morality:
only desire for money is proof
money's deserved:
only expected echoes
merit attention

    not generosities: that the one ('pointless')
    lights itself, its whole span,
    minute to minute, 'perception
    to perception,'—no crises
    dearly bought, forced up by leverage—
    but all of certain
    minutes of a certain life,

    while the other ('unplayable')
    lets you in—in!—to the presence of
    two, alone, who speak
    for a long time, a long
    time hardly moving,
    as people speak when alone, late, at last,
    at last speaking.

God knows there's enough
deprivation without
self-deprivation—because they tell you
the rules are broken! They gull you!
    Let your senses work, let
    your head have its head. The end
    is pleasure, and the heart
    of pleasure: enlightenment,
            mystery:

rhythm
       of their alternations, or best
       rarest and best,
                      their marriage—
a grace, fire, bread, what
keeps you moving, keeps your eyes
wide with seeing,
having something to see.

The Dogwood

The sink is full of dishes. Oh well.
Ten o'clock, there's no
hot water.
The kitchen floor is unswept, the broom
has been shedding straws. Oh well.

The cat is sleeping, Nikolai is sleeping,
Mitch is sleeping, early to bed,
aspirin for a cold. Oh well.

No school tomorrow, someone for lunch,
4 dollars left from the 10—how did that go?
Mostly on food. Oh well.

I could decide
to hear some chamber music
and today I saw—what?
Well, some huge soft deep
blackly gazing purple
and red (and pale)
anemones. Does that

take my mind off the dishes?
And dogwood besides.
Oh well. Early to bed, and I'll get up
early and put
a shine on everything and write
a letter to Duncan later that will shine too
with moonshine. Can I make it? Oh well.

Merritt Parkway

As if it were
forever that they move, that we
keep moving—

Under a wan sky where
as the lights went on a star
pierced the haze & now
follows steadily
a constant
above our six lanes
the dreamlike continuum . . .

And the people—ourselves!
the humans from inside the
cars, apparent
only at gasoline stops
unsure,
eyeing each other

               drink coffee hastily at the
         slot machines & hurry
     back to the cars
         vanish
         into them forever, to
         keep moving—

Houses now & then beyond the
sealed road, the trees / trees, bushes
passing by, passing
         the cars that
               keep moving ahead of
         us, past us, pressing behind us
                              and
                  over left, those that come
         toward us shining too brightly
moving relentlessly

     in six lanes, gliding
   north & south, speeding with
   a slurred sound—

                                        Something

'Something to
nullify the tall women on Madison
sniffing, peering at windows, sharp-eyed,
the ones with
little hope beyond the next hat?'

'Unequal forces.'

        'But unmeasured.
That the whirlpool remains
    (tossing aside the 'Around Manhattan' boat)
that the rocks remain
snarling among dusty lawns—
that's something.
        It was you who leapt—'

'from Spuyten Duyvil into
the desert!'

      'Into another whirlpool,
the pit of it, where money
rattles against the rocks as it's sucked down.
If it's a battle I'll take sides.'

        'But
not with nature—she won't fight—not
this battle. There's no
sequence, beyond that they both exist as
elements of a city: your whirlpool, and my
boars stuffed with dollar bills, "alive"
only with maggots.'

        'What then?'

'Whatever's animated: *that* fights back. Not
the neurotic thrust at subway doors
but, well, like the kids from Junior High
yelling when they let 'em out, chattering in
quick Spanish. Their faces change
from moment to moment
both the beautiful ones and those
deformed by want.
They yell and stamp

and cuff and wallop and shriek
as the bus sways off with them
and some before the enraged monitor
risk death each day
                 to cling to the backs of trucks, waving, and some
are grave, demure, but have earrings that shine & tremble.'

'You're almost lyrical!' 'Oh listen! It's
as if in their violent joy they were almost
about to be silent—all at once—
and weep in concourse.'

'And the minotaur will devour them.
It's life against death, and
                          death wins—
and will uproot the rocks, too, for pastime.'

'Deformed life, rather:
the maskfaced buyers of bric-a-brac
are the detritus only—of a
ferocious energy—'

                  'A monster.
Greed, is it? Alive, yes—'

'Whose victims
multiply quicker than it eats
and stubbornly
               flourish in the shadow of it.'

                                    Turning

The shifting, the shaded
    change of pleasure

Soft warm ashes in place of fire
    out, irremediably

and a door blown open:

planes tilt, interact, objects
    fuse, disperse,
    this chair further from that table . . . hold it!
    Focus on that: this table
    closer to that shadow. It's what appalls the
    heart's red rust. Turn, turn!
    Loyalty betrays.

        It's the fall of it, the drift,
            pleasure
        source and sequence
            lift
        of golden cold sea.

The Bereaved

. . . Could not speak
        could not speak
            no meeting was possible.

    We spoke without euphemism of their deaths
cheerfully of their lives.
At night a touch on the shoulder, wishes for sleep:
    no more. The children were dead.

Of one: he had grown thoughtful of late,
        read much, listened at night,
            was happy alone, but a sought companion.

64

The other:
certain words delighted her to laughter
her ways were quick and light.

No more.
Could not speak . . .

We could not speak:
a recoil from the abyss?
Did she see the mountain?
did she see the terraced olive-field, sunmist in hollows?
was the water cold and clear on her tongue?
the bucket risen
heavy
out of the black well-hole—
did she tremble before it?

The abyss was there.
(Standing there
she sees them darken and fall.)
We did not touch her
(she may not have seen us)
by fear or wisdom
did not touch her . . .

She left early
before violets opened
under the crumbled wall.

The Instant

'We'll go out before breakfast, and get
some mushrooms,' says my mother.

Early, early: the sun
risen, but hidden in mist

the square house left behind
sleeping, filled with sleepers;

up the dewy hill, quietly, with baskets.

Mushrooms firm, cold;
      tussocks of dark grass, gleam of webs,
turf soft and cropped. Quiet and early. And no valley,

no hills: clouds about our knees, tendrils
of cloud in our hair. Wet scrags
of wool caught in barbed wire, gorse
looming, without scent.
                    Then ah! suddenly
the lifting of it, the mist rolls
      quickly away, and far, far—

'Look!' she grips me, 'It is
           Eryri!
                It's Snowdon, fifty
      miles away!'—the voice
a wave rising to Eryri,
falling.
         Snowdon, home
of eagles, resting place of
Merlin, core of Wales.

           Light
graces the mountainhead
for a lifetime's look, before the mist
      draws in again.

'The dread word has been spoken.
I expect, like myself, you have known it
all along. He does not guess it, I think,
and yet . . .' And yet he knows it. *'We live*
from day to day, not
dipping too far
below the surface, and therefore
quite happily.
           You, too,
be happy, dear children' . . . So be it:
bow the head for once. Shall it be
in the red
almost-invisible spiders circling
a hot stone I shall take pleasure today?
The veery
          hidden, his song
     rippling downward, inward, over and over,
almost-visible spiral?

                  More:
let there be more joy!—if that
is what you would have. I dance
now that work's over and the house quiet:
alone among fireflies on the
dark lawn, humming and leaping.
'After all, life
is a journey to this goal
from the outset.' And Mr. Despondency's daughter
Muchafraid, went through the water singing?
                  I dance
for joy, only for joy
while you lie dying, into whose eyes
I looked seldom enough, all the years,
seldom with candid love. Let my dance

be mourning then,
now that I love you too late.

From desire to desire
                     plucking
white petals away from their
green centres.   *It was thus and thus*
repeats the head, the fantasist.
                        No matter:
that wind sweeps forward
again—life itself.
       Gather them, flawed, curled
       veined like a child's temple
       heaped one on another
                    irregular
displaced at a breath: secrets . . .
            So
one smiled, another turned pages:
steady, heartbeats apart; many
continuing variously—
And the stripped green? Alert, hard
on a thick stalk. So.

Shout into leaping wind
alone by spring lakes

On muddy paths, yellow grass
stamp, laugh; no one
to hear.

The water, water, dazzles;
                              dark winds
pluck its feathers
        splash the hissing reeds.
Birches lean on the air.

Lean into solitude
you whose joy is a kite
now dragged in dirt, now
breaking the ritual of sky.

Nice House

How charming, the colored cushions
curtains of brocade, the fine baskets
filled with fruit, candy, logs for the fire!

It was well-praised and well-shared, Nice House.
And so, many years passed. Hyacinths
in the garden, whiskey
never wanting, music of course.

And many years passed.

One day, came from the terrace and saw
the faded rags, curls of
dust blowing softly
across and across the room. Yes, correct,
brown flowers, smoking fire, the garbage

tipping out of its bag in the kitchen.
      The smell was probably mice.

It seemed the place was empty
at first—then we made out
the police, their black clothes in the shadows
waiting. The chief sat feet apart
beeksteak hands on his knees.
Nobody said a word—only
the lonely icebox set up its sobbing and shaking
which gave us cover, anyway.

A Supermarket in Guadalajara, Mexico

In the supermercado the music
    sweet as the hot afternoon
wanders among the watermelons,
    the melons, the sumptuous tomatoes,
and lingers among the tequila bottles,
    rum bacardi, rompope. It
hovers like flies round the butchers
    handsome and gay, as they dreamily
sharpen their knives; and the beautiful
    girl cashiers, relaxed
in the lap of the hot afternoon,
    breathe in time to the music
whether they know it or not—
    at the glossy supermercado,
the super supermercado.

A Song

Red flowers on a leafless tree.

All day the light is clear
the baker boy with his basket
comes and goes in the sun
his bicycle shines in the sun.

Red flowers on a leafless tree.

The dust of the fields is blowing
the cattle are eating dust and grass
all day the light is clear
the flowers shine in the sun.

Red flowers, shine for me.
The dust is gray and comforts me
a woolen blanket of soft dust.
I want your red to anger me.

The Recognition

Since the storm two nights ago
the air
is water-clear, the mountains
tranquil and clear.
              Have you seen
an intelligent invalid—that look
about the eyes and temples?—one who
knows damn well
death is coming—in the guise let's say

71

of a carpenter, coming
to fix him for good
with his big hammer and
sharp nails.
                    The air and the horizon.
Clouds make
        gestures of flight but
remain suspended. The builders
continue to build the
house next door.
                Nothing
will happen. A transparence
of the flesh, revealing
not bones but the shape of bones.

Scenes from the Life of the Peppertrees

i

The peppertrees, the peppertrees!

Cats are stretching in the doorways,
sure of everything. It is morning.
    But the peppertrees
stand aside in diffidence, with berries
of modest red.
                Branch above branch, an air
of lightness; of shadows
scattered lightly.
                A cat
closes upon its shadow.
Up and up goes the sun,
sure of everything.
        The peppertrees
                shiver a little.

Robust
and soot-black, the cat
leaps to a low branch. Leaves
close about him.

ii

The yellow moon dreamily
tipping buttons of light
down among the leaves. Marimba,
marimba—from beyond the
black street.
                    Somebody dancing,
somebody
              getting the hell
outta here. Shadows of cats
weave round the tree trunks,
the exposed knotty roots.

iii

The man on the bed sleeping
defenseless. Look—
his bare long feet together
sideways, keeping each other
warm. And the foreshortened shoulders,
the head
barely visible.   He is good.
let him sleep.
              But the third peppertree
    is restless, twitching
thin leaves in the light
of afternoon.   After a while
it walks over and taps
on the upstairs window with a bunch
of red berries.   Will he wake?

73

The Sharks

Well then, the last day the sharks appeared.
Dark fins appear, innocent
as if in fair warning. The sea becomes
sinister, are they everywhere?
I tell you, they break six feet of water.
Isn't it the same sea, and won't we
play in it any more?
I liked it clear and not
too calm, enough waves
to fly in on. For the first time
I dared to swim out of my depth.
It was sundown when they came, the time
when a sheen of copper stills the sea,
not dark enough for moonlight, clear enough
to see them easily. Dark
the sharp lift of the fins.

Action

I can lay down that history
I can lay down my glasses
I can lay down the imaginary lists
of what to forget and what must be
done. I can shake the sun
out of my eyes and lay everything down
on the hot sand, and cross
the whispering threshold and walk
right into the clear sea, and float there,
my long hair floating, and fishes
vanishing all around me. Deep water.

Little by little one comes to know
the limits and depths of power.

Lonely Man

An open world
        within its mountain rim:
trees on the plain lifting
        their heads, fine strokes
        of grass stretching themselves to breathe
the last of the light.
                        Where a man
riding horseback raises dust
        under the eucalyptus trees, a long way off, the dust
is gray-gold, a cloud
        of pollen. A field
        of cosmea turns
        all its many faces
of wide-open flowers west, to the light.

It is your loneliness
your energy
            baffled in the stillness
        gives an edge to the shadows—
the great sweep of mountain shadow,
shadows of ants and leaves,
        the stones of the road each with its shadow
and you with your long shadow
closing your book and standing up
to stretch, your long shadow-arms
        stretching back of you, baffled.

The kitchen patio in snowy
moonlight.   That
snowsilence, that
abandon to stillness.
The sawhorse, the concrete
washtub, snowblue. The washline
bowed under its snowfur!
Moon has silenced
the crickets, the summer frogs
hold their breath.
Summer night, summer night, standing
one-legged, a crane
in the snowmarsh, staring
at snowmoon!

Pure Products

To the sea they came—
2000 miles in an old bus
fitted with brittle shelves and makeshift beds
and cluttered with U.S. canned goods
                        —to the Sea!
on which they paddle
innertubes   —and the lowhovering Sun!
from which the old woman hides her head
under what looks like
a straw wastebasket.
                        'Yep, they cured me all right,
but see, it made my breasts grow like a woman's.'
And she: 'Something hurts him in his chest,

76

I think
        maybe it's his heart,'—and hers
I can see beating at the withered throat.

To the Sea some force has driven them—
        away from a lifetime.
And in this windless heat they purpose
to walk the 3 miles of shadeless beach to the store
to ask in Spanish (of which they know
only yes and no) for wholewheat flour
(which is unknown in the region) that she
may bake their bread!
                They are dying
in their gentleness, adorned
with wrinkled apple smiles—nothing
remains for them
but to live a little, invoking
the old powers.

Illustrious Ancestors

The Rav
of Northern White Russia declined,
in his youth, to learn the
language of birds, because
the extraneous did not interest him; nevertheless
when he grew old it was found
he understood them anyway, having
listened well, and as it is said, 'prayed
                with the bench and the floor.' He used
what was at hand—as did
Angel Jones of Mold, whose meditations
were sewn into coats and britches.

Well, I would like to make,
thinking some line still taut between me and them,
poems direct as what the birds said,
hard as a floor, sound as a bench,
mysterious as the silence when the tailor
would pause with his needle in the air.

Broken Glass

Two bean-fed boys set bottles on the wall
yesterday, and shied at them for a half-hour
with desperate energy, taking their stand
back a way in the rubbled lot.
Now the green fragments glitter.
Is that a lizard stirred among them?
The black goat that goes ahead of the cows
picks by in a hurry, her udders rocking.
She hears
            something I don't hear.
The young ivy leaves
are shining. Is it spring?

Sunday Afternoon

After the First Communion
and the banquet of mangoes and
bridal cake, the young daughters
of the coffee merchant lay down
for a long siesta, and their white dresses

lay beside them in quietness
and the white veils floated
in their dreams as the flies buzzed.
But as the afternoon
burned to a close they rose
and ran about the neighborhood
among the halfbuilt villas
alive, alive, kicking a basketball, wearing
other new dresses, of bloodred velvet.

The Lesson

Martha, 5, scrawling a drawing, murmurs
'These are two angels. These are two bombs. They
are in the sunshine. Magic
is dropping from the angels' wings.'
Nik, at 4, called
        over the stubble field, 'Look,
the flowers are dancing underneath the
tree, and the tree
        is looking down with all its apple-eyes.'
Without hesitation or debate, words
used and at once forgotten.

The Whirlwind

The doors keep rattling—I
stick poems between their teeth to
stop them. The brown dust

twirls up outside the window, off
the dead jicama field, scares the curtains,
spirals away to the dirty hollow
where the cesspools are, and the most ants,
and beyond—to the unfenced pasture land, where nothing
will get in its way for miles and it
can curtsey itself at last into
some arroyo.   The doors
keep rattling—I'm
shivering, desperate for a poem
to stuff into their maws that will
silence them. I know what they want:
they want
in all their wooden strength
to fly off on the whirlwind into
the great nothingness.

A Stir in the Air

A stir in the air, the proper space
holding existences in grave distinction—
If as you read I walk
          around you in a
                half circle
your response to the poem will
waver, maybe, like the lights just now
in the thunderstorm—the balance
is that fine—the dance
of hiving bees it is, that design
in air, joyfully
          reducing possibilities to
                              one, the next act.

80

The Absence

Here I lie asleep
or maybe I'm awake yet—

not alone—and yet
it seems by moonlight

I'm alone, hardly hearing
a breath beside me. And those shadows

on the wall indeed are
not shadows but the
featherweight dancing echoes
of headlights sliding by.

Here I lie and wonder
what it is has left me, what element.
I can't remember my dreams
by morning.
          Maybe, as Frazer tells,

my soul flew out in that moment
of almost-sleep.   If it should go
back to the scenes and times
of its wars and losses

how would I ever lure it
back? It would

be looking for something, it would be
too concentrated to hear me.

O moon, watching everything,
delay it in the garden among the white flowers

until the cold air before sunrise
makes it glad to come back to me through the screens.

The red eyes of rabbits
aren't sad. No one passes
the sad golden village in a barge
any more. The sunset
will leave it alone. If the
curtains hang askew
it is no one's fault.
Around and around and around
everywhere the same sound
of wheels going, and things
growing older, growing
silent. If the dogs
bark to each other
all night, and their eyes
flash red, that's
nobody's business. They have
a great space of dark to
bark across. The rabbits
will bare their teeth at
the spring moon.

WITH EYES AT THE BACK OUR HEADS (1960)

The Artist

(*From the Spanish translation of Toltec Códice de la Real Academia, fol. 315, v. With the help of Elvira Abascal who understood the original Toltec.*)

The artist: disciple, abundant, multiple, restless.
The true artist: capable, practicing, skillful;
maintains dialogue with his heart, meets things with his
*   mind.*

The true artist: draws out all from his heart,
works with delight, makes things with calm, with sagacity,
works like a true Toltec, composes his objects, works
*   dexterously, invents;*
arranges materials, adorns them, makes them adjust.

The carrion artist: works at random, sneers at the people,
makes things opaque, brushes across the surface of the face
*   of things,*
works without care, defrauds people, is a thief.

El Artista

El artista: discípulo, abundante, múltiple, inquieto.
El verdadero artista: capaz, se adiestra, es hábil;
dialoga con su corazón, encuentra las cosas con su mente.

El verdadero artista todo lo saca de su corazón,
obra con deleite, hace las cosas con calma, con tiento,
obra como un tolteca, compone cosas, obra hábilmente, crea;
arregla las cosas, las hace atildadas, hace que se ajusten.

El torpe artista: obra al azar, se burla de la gente,
opaca las cosas, pasa por encima del rostro de la cosas,
obra sin cuidado, defrauda a las personas, es un ladrón.

Toltecatl

In toltecatl; tlamachtilli, tolih, centozon, aman.
In qualli toltecatl: mozcaliani, mozcaliz, mihmati;
moyolnonotzani, tlalnamiquini.

In qualli toltecatl tlayollocopaviani,
tlapaccachivani, tlaiviyanchivani, tlamavhcachiva,
toltecati, tlatalia, tlahimati, tlayocoya;—
tlavipana, tlapopotia, tlananamictia.

In xolopihtli toltecatl; tlailivizviani, teca mocayavani,
tlaixpachoani, iixco quihquiza,
tlailivizvia, teca mocayava, ichtequi.

With eyes at the back of our heads
we see a mountain
not obstructed with woods but laced
here and there with feathery groves.

The doors before us in a façade
that perhaps has no house in back of it
are too narrow, and one is set high
with no doorsill. The architect sees

the imperfect proposition and
turns eagerly to the knitter.
Set it to rights!
The knitter begins to knit.

For we want
to enter the house, if there is a house,
to pass through the doors at least
into whatever lies beyond them,

we want to enter the arms
of the knitted garment. As one
is re-formed, so the other,
in proportion.

When the doors widen
when the sleeves admit us
the way to the mountain will clear,
the mountain we see with
eyes at the back of our heads, mountain
green, mountain
cut of limestone, echoing
with hidden rivers, mountain
of short grass and subtle shadows.

Returning

      to all the unsaid
all the lost living untranslated
in any sense,
and the dead
unrecognized, celebrated
only in dreams that die by morning

is a mourning or ghostwalking only.
        You must make, said music

    in its voices of metal and wood
in its dancing diagrams, moving
apart and together, along
      and over and under a line
and speaking in one voice,

           make
my image.   Let be
what is gone.

The Departure

Have you got the moon safe?
Please, tie those strings a little tighter.
This loaf, push it down further
the light is crushing it—such a baguette
golden brown and so white inside
you don't see every day

87

nowadays. And for God's sake
don't let's leave in the end
without the ocean! Put it
in there among the shoes, and
tie the moon on behind. It's time!

The Five-Day Rain

The washing hanging from the lemon tree
in the rain
and the grass long and coarse.

Sequence broken, tension
of sunlight broken.
                            So light a rain

fine shreds
pending above the rigid leaves.

Wear scarlet! Tear the green lemons
off the tree!   I don't want
to forget who I am, what has burned in me
and hang limp and clean, an empty dress—

The Dead Butterfly

i

Now I see its whiteness
is not white but green, traced with green,

and resembles the stones
of which the city is built,
quarried high in the mountains.

ii

Everywhere among the marigolds
the rainblown roses and the hedges
of tamarisk are white
butterflies this morning, in constant
tremulous movement, only those
that lie dead revealing
their rockgreen color and the bold
cut of the wings.

The Lost Black-and-White Cat

Cockcrowing at midnight.   Broken
silence. Crickets skillfully re-
forming it in
                        minims and
quavers.   The child turns, bangs
        the headboard, struggles
with dreams. Last night in dreams
he found the cat in the bathroom.

                Come back, cat.
Thrash the silence with your autonomous
feather tail. Imagination made fur,
come back, spring poems out of the whole
cloth of silence.

89

This lagoon with its glass shadows
and naked golden shallows
the mangrove island, home of white herons,

recalls the Loire at La Charité
that ran swiftly in quiet ripples
brimful of clouds from the evening sky.

In both, the presence of a rippling quiet
    limpid over the sandbars, suspended,
    and drawing over the depths
long lines of beveled darkness,
draws the mind
down to its own depths

where the imagination swims,
shining dark-scaled fish,
swims and waits, flashes, waits and
wavers, shining of its own light.

Pleasures

I like to find
what's not found
at once, but lies

within something of another nature,
in repose, distinct.
Gull feathers of glass, hidden

in white pulp: the bones of squid
which I pull out and lay
blade by blade on the draining board—

    tapered as if for swiftness, to pierce
    the heart, but fragile, substance
    belying design.   Or a fruit, *mamey,*

cased in rough brown peel, the flesh
rose-amber, and the seed:
the seed a stone of wood, carved and

polished, walnut-colored, formed
like a brazilnut, but large,
large enough to fill
the hungry palm of a hand.

I like the juicy stem of grass that grows
within the coarser leaf folded round,
and the butteryellow glow
in the narrow flute from which the morning-glory
opens blue and cool on a hot morning.

The Offender

The eye luminous
in its box of ebony
saw the point of departure, a room
pleasant, bare, sunlit,
and space beyond it, time
extending to mountains, ending,
beginning new space beyond.

The eye, luminous, grayblue,
a moonstone,
brimmed over with mercury tears
that rolled and were lost in sunny dust.
The world in the lustre of a
black pupil moved its clouds
and their shadows. Time
had gathered itself and gone. The eye
luminous, prince of solitude.

Seems Like We Must Be Somewhere Else

Sweet procession, rose-blue,
and all them bells.

Bandstand red, the eyes
at treetop level seeing it. 'Are we
what we think we are or are we
what befalls us?'

The people from an open window
the eyes
seeing it!   Daytime!   Or twilight!

Sweet procession, rose-blue.
If we're here let's be here now.

And the train whistle? who
invented that? Lonesome man, wanted the trains
to speak for him.

Maybe it is true we have to return
to the black air of ashcan city
because it is there the most life was burned,

as ghosts or criminals return?
But no, the city has no monopoly
of intense life. The dust burned

golden or violet in the wide land
to which we ran away, images
of passion sprang out of the land

as whirlwinds or red flowers, your hands
opened in anguish or clenched in violence
under that sun, and clasped my hands

in that place to which we will not return
where so much happened that no one else noticed,
where the city's ashes that we brought with us
flew into the intense sky still burning.

Triple Feature

Innocent decision: to enjoy.
And the pathos
of hopefulness, of his solicitude:

—he in mended serape,
she having plaited carefully
magenta ribbons into her hair,
the baby a round half-hidden shape

slung in her rebozo, and the young son steadfastly
gripping a fold of her skirt,
pale and severe under a
handed-down sombrero—

           all regarding
the stills with full attention, preparing
to pay and go in—
to worlds of shadow-violence, half-
familiar, warm with popcorn, icy
with strange motives, barbarous splendors!

A Letter

I know you will come, bringing me
an opal. Good! I will come
to meet you. And walk back with you
to meet whatever it is raves to us
for release.   New courage
has stirred in me while you were gone.
They are stripping the bark from the trees
to make soup
and sitting down I crush fifty
blackeyed susans, each no bigger than a
one-cent piece.   I'm tired
of all that is not mine. Lighting
two cigarettes by mistake, lying back
one in each hand, surprised,
Buddha of the anthill. A great day!
The first to waken as a bear
from cosy smelly comfort ("a rock
dressed in brown moss, little eyes
glinting") and walk out
to the hunt.

94

Another Journey

From a world composed, closed to us,
back to nowhere, the north.
                            We need
a cold primrose sting
of east wind; we need
a harsh design of magic lights at night over
drab streets, tears
salting our mouths, whether the east wind
brought them or the jabbing
of memories and perceptions, who knows.
                   Not history, but our own histories,
a brutal dream drenched with our lives,
intemperate, open, illusory,

     to which we wake, sweating to make
substance of it, grip it, turn
its face to us, unwilling, and see the
snowflakes glitter there, and melt.

The Take Off

The mountains through the shadowy
flickering of the propellers, steady,
melancholy, relaxed, indifferent, a world
lost to our farewells.
                  The rising of the smoke
from valleys, the pearly waters, the
tight-lipped brown fields, all is relaxed,
melancholy, steady, radiant with dawn stillness,
the world indivisible, from which we fly—

sparks, motes, flickers
of energy, willful, afraid, uttering
harsh interior cries, silent, waving and smiling to the
invisible guardians of our losses.

Girlhood of Jane Harrison

At a window—
so much is easy to see:

an outleaning from indoor darkness
to garden darkness.

But marzipan! Could so much sweetness
not seem banal?

No: it was a calling of
roses by other names.

Now from, as it may be,
the cedar tree

out went the points of the star.
The dance was a stamping in

of autumn. A dance in the garden
to welcome the fall. The diagram

was a diamond, like the pan
for star-cake.   Multiplied,

the dancer moved outward to all the
promontories of shadow, the

forest bays, the moon islands. With
roses of marzipan
the garden dissolved its boundaries.

A Happening

Two birds, flying East, hit the night
at three in the afternoon; stars came out
over the badlands and the billowy
snowlands; they floundered on
resolving not to turn back in search
of lost afternoon; continuing
through cotton wildernesses
through the stretched night
and caught up with dawn in a rainstorm
in the city, where they fell
in semblance of torn paper sacks
to the sidewalk on 42nd St., and resumed
their human shape, and separated:
one turned uptown, to follow
the Broadway river to its possible source,
the other downtown, to see
the fair and goodly harbor; but each,
accosted by shadows that muttered to him
pleading mysteriously, half-hostile, was drawn
into crosstown streets, into
revolving doorways, into nameless
small spaces back of buildings,
airless airshafts, till no more
was known of man, bird, nor paper.

When the mice awaken
and come out to their work of searching
for life, crumbs of life,
I sit quiet in my back room
trying to quiet my mind of its chattering,
rumors and events, and find
life, crumbs of life, to nourish it
until in stillness, replenished,
the animal god within the
cluttered shrine   speaks.   Alas!
poor mice—I have left
nothing for them, no bread,
no fat, not an unwashed plate.
Go through the walls to other kitchens;
let it be silent here.
I'll sit in vigil
awaiting the Cat
who with human tongue
speaks inhuman oracles
or delicately, with its claws, opens
Chinese boxes, each containing
the World and its shadow.

The Room

With a mirror
I could see the sky.

With two mirrors or three
justly placed, I could see
the sun bowing to the evening chimneys.

Moonrise—the moon itself might appear
in a fourth mirror placed high
and close to the open window.

        With enough mirrors within
and even without the room, a cantilever
supporting them, mountains
and oceans might be manifest.

I understand perfectly
that I could encounter my own eyes
too often—I take account
of the danger—
        If the mirrors
are large enough, and arranged
with bravura, I can look
beyond my own glance.

With one mirror
how many stars could I see?

I don't want to escape, only to see
the enactment of rites.

                            The Sage

The cat is eating the roses:
that's the way he is.
Don't stop him, don't stop
the world going round,
that's the way things are.
The third of May
was misty; fourth of May

who knows. Sweep
the rose-meat up, throw the bits
out in the rain.
He never eats
every crumb, says
the hearts are bitter.
That's the way he is, he knows
the world and the weather.

The Communion

A pondering frog looks
out from my eyes:

dark-red, veiled blue, plums
roll to the center of a bowl

and at close horizon water-towers
hump and perch.

                    Leap
frog, to a lake: leaves
support the lilies, water holds

erect the long, strong stems,
reflects gleaming

rosy petals, pollen-yellow lily-buds,
clouds lilac-tinted and dissolving.
Back to the plums—

eggs in a blue nest—the squat
peaked assembly of towers.

What is it?
      An accord.

Break out, frog,
sing, you who don't know

anything about anything.
'To dance without moving' shall be your burden.

February Evening in New York

As the stores close, a winter light
   opens air to iris blue,
     glint of frost through the smoke,
     grains of mica, salt of the sidewalk.
As the buildings close, released autonomous
   feet pattern the streets
     in hurry and stroll; balloon heads
     drift and dive above them; the bodies
     aren't really there.
As the lights brighten, as the sky darkens,
   a woman with crooked heels says to another woman
   while they step along at a fair pace,
   'You know, I'm telling you, what I love best
   is life. I love life! Even if I ever get
   to be old and wheezy—or limp! You know?
   Limping along?—I'd still . . .' Out of hearing.
To the multiple disordered tones
   of gears changing, a dance
   to the compass points, out, four-way river.
   Prospect of sky
   wedged into avenues, left at the ends of streets,
   west sky, east sky: more life tonight! A range
   of open time at winter's outskirts.

Its form speaks of gliding
    though one had never seen a swan

      and strands of silver, caught
      in the branches near it, speak

of rain suspended in a beam of light,

      one speech conjuring the other.

      All trivial parts of
      world-about-us speak in their forms
      of themselves and their counterparts!

Rain glides aslant,
   swan pauses in mid-stroke,
      stamped on the mind's light, but aloof—

and the eye that sees them refuses
to see further, glances off the
surfaces that
          speak and conjure,
rests

      on the frail
      strawness of straw, metal sheen of tinsel.

      How far might one go
      treading the cleft the swan cut?

The Dead

Earnestly I looked
into their abandoned faces
at the moment of death and while
I bandaged their slack jaws and
straightened waxy unresistant limbs and plugged
the orifices with cotton
but like everyone else I learned
each time nothing new, only that
as it were, a music, however harsh, that held us
however loosely, had stopped, and left
a heavy thick silence in its place.

Notes of a Scale

i

A noon with twilight overtones
from open windows looking down.
Hell! it goes by. The trees
practice green in faithful measure.
It could be what I'm waiting for is
not here at all. Yet
the trees have it, don't they?
Absorbed in their own magic,
abundant, hermetic, wide open.

ii

The painting within itself,
a boy that has learned to whistle,

a fisherman. The painting
living its magic, admitting
nothing, being, the boy
pushing his hands further into his
pockets, the fisherman
beginning the day, in dew and half-dark,
by a river whose darkness
will be defined as brown in a
half-hour. The painting
suspended in itself, an angler
in the suspense of daybreak,
whistling to itself.

iii

Where the noon passes
in camouflage of twilight

doesn't cease to look
into it from his oblique
angle, leafwise,
'. . . maintains dialog with his heart,'

doesn't spill the beans
balances like a papaya tree on a single
young elephant-leg.

iv

A glass brimming, not spilling,
the green trees
practising their art.
     'A wonder
  from the true world,'
he who accomplished it

104

'overwhelmed with the wonder
which rises out of his doing.'

Note: See 'The True Wonder,' anecdote of Rabbi Elimélekh of
Lijensk in Buber's *Tales of the Hasidim: The Early Masters*

Terror

Face-down; odor
of dusty carpet. The grip
of anguished stillness.

Then your naked voice, your
head knocking the wall, sideways,
the beating of trapped thoughts against iron.

If I remember, how is it
my face shows
barely a line? Am I
a monster, to sing
in the wind on this sunny hill

and not taste the dust always,
and not hear
that rending, that retching?
How did morning come, and the days
that followed, and quiet nights?

i

Shells, husks, the wandering
of autumn seeds, the loitering
of curled indoor leaves holding
by a cobweb to the bark
many days before falling.

Cracking husk, afraid
it may reveal a dirty emptiness
afraid its hazelnut may be green,
bitter, of no account.

. . . .

Seed, cling
to the hard earth, some footstep
will grind you in,

new leaf, open your green hand,
old leaf, fall and rot
enriching your rich brotherhood,

hazelnut, know when ripeness
has hardened you and sweetened you.

ii

To shed this fake face
as a snakeskin, paper
dragon the winds will tear—
to dig shame up, a buried bone
and tie it to my breast—

(would it change, in time,
to an ornament? Could it serve
to be carved with new designs?)

iii

I look among your papers
for something that will give you to me
until you come back;
and find: *'Where are my dreams?'*

Your dreams! Have they not nourished my life?
Didn't I poach among them, as now on your desk?
My cheeks grown red and my hair curly
as I roasted your pheasants by my night fire!
    My dreams are gone off to hunt yours,
I won't take them back unless they find yours,
they must return torn by your forests.

Unremembered
                our dreams move together
in our dark heads, wander
in landscapes unlit by our candle eyes
eyes of self love and self disgust
eyes of your love for me kindling my cold heart
eyes of my love for you flickering at the edge of you.

iv

Among the tall elders of the hereafter
my father had become
                a blissful foolish rose
his face beaming from among petals
(of sunset pink) 'open as a daisy'—
a rose walking, tagging at the heels

of the wise, having found
a true form.

v

The tree of life is growing
in a corner of the living-room
held to its beam by nails
that encircle, not pierce, its stem.
From its first shoots, many leaves,
then a long, curved, and back-curving bare stretch,
and above, many leaves, many new shoots,
spreading left along the wall, and right,
towards your worktables.

Casals' cello (a live broadcast: the resistances
                    of the live bow, the passion manifest
                    in living hands, not smoothed out on wax)
speaks from across the room
and the tree of life answers
with its green silence and apparent stillness.

The cello is hollow and the stems are hollow.
The space of the cello is shaped; no other form would
        resound
with the same tones; the stems at their branchings-off
widen, and narrow to a new growth.
As bow touches strings, a voice is heard;
at the articulations of green, a path
moves toward a leaf. There is space in us

but the lines and planes of its form
are what we reach for and fall,
touching nothing (outside ourselves and yet
                    standing somewhere within our own
                        space,
                    in its darkness).

108

Buds are knots in our flesh, nodules of pain.

What holds us upright, once we have faced
immeasurable darkness, the black point
at our eyes' center? Were we suspended,
museum butterflies, by a filament, from a hidden nail?
Has it broken when we begin to
fall, slowly, without desire?
(But we don't fall. The floor is flat, the round earth
is flat, and we stand on it, and though we lie down
and fill our lungs with choking dust
and spread our arms to make a cross
after a while we rise and creep away,
walk from one room to another
'on our feet again.')

Your worktable
is close to the tree—not a tree perhaps,
a vine.
In time the leaves
will reach the space above it, between the windows.

Cello and vine commune
in the space of a room.

What will speak to you?
What notes of abundance
strike across the living room
to your bowed head and down-curved back?

Watch the beloved vine. We can't
see it move.

Listen, listen . . .
We are in this room
together. You are alone
forming darkness into words

dark on white paper,
I am alone with the sense of your anguish.
The tree of life is growing in the room,
the living-room, the work-room.

vi

Between the white louvers, nectarine
light, and on the carpet's earthbrown, amber,
entered, filled unpeopled space with presence.
From the doorway we saw
harmonies and heard
measured colors of light, not quite awake and so awake
to correspondences. A room in a house in the city
became for a space of fine, finely-drawn,
November morning, a Holy Apple Field.

And from the table to the crimson
blanket, from the other, carved, table
to the ashes of last night's fire, slanted
louvered light, passing without haste.
We watched from the doorway between sleeping and
    waking.
Green to the white ceiling drew the vine.

The Goddess

She in whose lipservice
I passed my time,
whose name I knew, but not her face,
came upon me where I lay in Lie Castle!

110

Flung me across the room, and
room after room (hitting the walls, re-
bounding—to the last
sticky wall—wrenching away from it
pulled hair out!)
till I lay
outside the outer walls!

There in cold air
lying still where her hand had thrown me,
I tasted the mud that splattered my lips:
the seeds of a forest were in it,
asleep and growing! I tasted
her power!

The silence was answering my silence,
a forest was pushing itself
out of sleep between my submerged fingers.

I bit on a seed and it spoke on my tongue
of day that shone already among stars
in the water-mirror of low ground,
and a wind rising ruffled the lights:
she passed near me returning from the encounter,
she who plucked me from the close rooms,

without whom nothing
flowers, fruits, sleeps in season,
without whom nothing
speaks in its own tongue, but returns
lie for lie!

Under an orange-tree—
not one especial singular
orange-tree, but one among

the dark multitude. Recline
there, with a stone winejar

and the sense
of another dream
concentration would capture—
but it doesn't matter—

and the sense
of dust on the grass, of infinitesimal
flowers, of
cracks in the earth

and urgent life
passing there, ants and transparent
winged beings in their intensity
traveling from blade to blade,

under a modest orange-tree
neither lower nor taller
neither darker-leaved nor aglow
more beneficently

than the dark multitude
glowing in numberless lanes
the orange-farmer counts, but
not you—recline

and drink wine—the stone
will keep it cold—with the sense

112

of life yet to be lived—rest, rest,
the grass is growing—

let the oranges
ripen, ripen above you,
you are living too, one
among the dark multitude—

Fritillary

A chequered lily,
fritillary, named
for a dicebox, shall be
our emblem

and the butterfly
so like it one would see
a loose petal blowing
if it flew over
              where the flowers grew.

A field flower
but rare,
chequered dark and light,

and its winged semblance
lapsing from sky to earth,

fritillary, a chance word
speaking of glancing shadows, of
flying fluttering delights, to be

our talisman in sorrow.

A frog under you,
knees drawn up
ready to leap out of time,

a dog beside you,
snuffing at you, seeking
scent of you, an idea unformulated,

I give up on
trying to answer my question,
Do I love you enough?

It's enough to be
so much here. And
certainly when I catch

your mind in the
act of plucking
truth from the dark surrounding nowhere

as a swallow skims a
gnat from the
deep sky,

I don't stop to ask myself
Do I love him? but
laugh for joy.

How much I should like to begin
a poem with And—presupposing
the hardest said—
the moss cleared off the stone,
the letters plain.
How the round moon
would shine into all the corners
of such a poem and show
the words! Moths and dazzled
awakened birds
would freeze in its light!
The lines would be
an outbreak of bells
and I swinging on the rope!

Yet, not desiring apocrypha
but true revelation,
what use to pretend the stone discovered,
anything visible?
That poem indeed
may not be carved there, may lie
—the quick of mystery—
in animal eyes gazing
from the thicket,
a creature of unknown size,
fierce, terrified, having teeth or
no defense, but whom
no And may approach suddenly.

Way out there where words jump
in the haze
is the land of hot mamas.

Or say, in the potato patch
a million bugs glittering green and bronze
climb up and down the stems
exchanging perceptions.

     I in my balloon
light where the wind
permits a landing,
in my own province.

The Great Dahlia

Great lion-flower, whose flames
are tipped with white,
so it seems each petal's fire
burns out in snowy ash,

a dawn bird will light
on the kitchen table
to sing at midday for you

and have you noticed?
a green spider came with you
from the garden where they cut you,
to be the priest of your temple.

116

Burn, burn the day. The wind
is trying to enter and praise you.
Silence seems something you have chosen,
withholding your bronze voice.
We bow before your pride.

Bread

As florid berries to the oak, should I pin
sequins to this Rockland County bouquet
of bare twigs?—as roses
to pineboughs?—While a primrose-yellow
apple, flushed with success, levitates quietly
in the top right-hand corner of a small canvas,
giving pleasure by its happiness?
But these are thin pleasures, to content
the contented. For hunger:
the bare stretching thorny branches that may never speak
though they conceal or half-reveal
sharp small syllables of bud; and the ragged laughter
—showing gaps between its teeth—
of the anonymous weeds, tousle-heads,
yellow-brown like the draggled undersides of
dromedary and llama basking
proud and complete in airy wedges
of April sun—something
of endurance, to endure
ripeness if it come, or suffer
a slow spring with lifted head—
a good crust of brown bread for the hungry.

That dog with daisies for eyes
who flashes forth
flame of his very self at every bark
is the Dog of Art.
Worked in wool, his blind eyes
look inward to caverns and jewels
which they see perfectly,
and his voice
measures forth the treasure
in music sharp and loud,
sharp and bright,
bright flaming barks,
and growling smoky soft, the Dog
of Art turns to the world
the quietness of his eyes.

A Dream

A story was told me of the sea, of time suspended as calm
seas balance and hover, of a breaking and hastening of time
in sea tempest, of slow oil-heavy time turning its engines
over in a sultry night at sea. The story belonged not to time
but to the sea; its time and its men were of the sea, the sea
held them, and the sea itself was bounded by darkness.

The man who told it was young when it began—a young
ship's officer on that ship whose name he did not tell.

Among the crew—many of whom had sailed together
many times before the young officer joined them—were two,
Antonio and Sabrinus, who were regarded by the rest with
a peculiar respectful affection.

118

These two were friends; and in the harmony of their responses, their communing quietness, seemed twin brothers, more than friends.

Their friendship, while it enclosed them in its ring, did not arouse jealousy or contempt; a gentle and serene light glowed out from it and was seen as something fair and inviolable.

The Captain himself (rarely seen on deck) allowed them a special privilege: In an idle time Antonio had built with matchless skill a small boat of his own, which when completed he and Sabrinus painted a glowing red, not scarlet but bright carmine. This—slight and elegant as a shelf model, but fully seaworthy—Antonio was permitted to keep in special davits; and when the ship anchored in roads or harbor, or lay becalmed in midvoyage, he and Sabrinus would go fishing in her—sailing if there were wind enough, or rowing at times of glassy lull.

Even this caused no resentment. That they seemed to share thoughts as well as words—not many of the men understood their language, which may have been Portuguese or Catalan, or some island dialect—and that the catboat or skiff held only two, was tacitly accepted. An unfailing gentleness and kindly composure compensated for their reserve.

As for daily work, the ship's life, Antonio and Sabrinus were quick, sagacious, and diligent.

Indeed the young man soon came to realize that a belief had grown among the men that Antonio and Sabrinus were luck-bringers and that no evil would come to them or to the ship as long as those two were there.

So that when one night (or it may have begun on a dark day) a storm came up that grew fiercer hour by hour, it appeared to them at first 'only' a storm. The wind became a thing, solid, heavily insistent, lacking only visibility—and yet remained only the wind; and the spring waves it whipped up, though they rose higher than the ship itself, and seemed about to devour everything they could reach, were still only waves; and confident that ship and voyage were under the protection of a special providence, manifested in the incandescent companionship of the holy friends, the crew staggered and gripped and moved as they could about the lunging decks without true fear.

But there was an end to this time of brave activity; for as life slid violently aside and back, and the storm achieved its very orgasm, a chill silent fear struck the men, at seeing Antonio and Sabrinus in a new aspect—hatred marking their faces and bitter words breaking out between them. The cause of the quarrel was the crimson boat. Antonio, believing the ship about to sink, determined to loose and launch his artifact, and counted on his friend to take his chance of life in her with him, frail though she was in such a sea. But it seemed less the chance of life he desired than to give his boat her freedom, so that if she were destroyed it would be in open combat with the great ocean, not as a prisoner bound fast to the body of the ship. And Sabrinus refused.

Though the greater number of the listening men surrounding them on three sides (on the fourth was the sea itself) could not understand their language, and those who did could catch only a few words from the storm's clamor, all understood that Sabrinus was saying, No, they must always as before stand by the ship to which they were committed, and help their fellows save her if they could—must share the common fate as if they were common men. Neither would be swayed by the other, and in a moment the two men, set apart in hatred as in love, set upon one another, oblivious of all that encircled them, in a murderous fight. As the young officer saw it, this hatred was the long-secreted flower of their love, the unsuspected fearful harvest of long calm voyages, of benevolent quietness and exclusive understandings.

Not a man but clung to whatever rail or stanchion he could find on the steep decks to see this abominable flowering, cold at heart. But no one thought for a moment of stepping between them, it was the storm itself intervened: as

Antonio and Sabrinus held one another in choking grip, the vessel was lifted in the sea's gleaming teeth. The deck shuddered and pitched them overboard into a great trough of the waters, as if to appease the great mouth.

Then the wind was no longer a thing, but an evil, multiple, personage; and the waves swept up upon them with intent of malice. The blessed cord that bound ship and men to happy fortune had broken. No one listened to what orders they could hear, the Captain vanished from the bridge, and in half an hour the ship had split and sunk. The survivors, reaching shore, dispersed, and of them the storyteller had no more to say.

But the story of Antonio and Sabrinus was not ended. This is what he told:

Many years later it happened that he found himself without a berth in an obscure, sleazy tropical port—perhaps in Central America, at all events in a hot, moist climate. Eager to get away from the sultry city, he shipped as first mate on the freighter *Jacobi* at very short notice, the officer he replaced having been taken seriously ill. The owners, only eager for the perishable cargo to reach its destination by a certain date, concealed from him the fact that there was fever aboard.

He joined the ship at dusk; by midnight they were well out to sea, and having soon become aware of the crew's depletion, he was musing angrily at the deception practiced on him, which the captain had shiftily admitted once they were out of port. A little after midnight he descended into the sick men's quarters.

The steaming darkness here was in sharp contrast to the bright moonlight he had just left. Dim lights swung here and there; crowded with hammocks and cramped bunks, the space in which these men were isolated seemed a hellish writhing mass of discolored and tormented forms.

He passed from one to another grimly inspecting the disorder, flashing a shielded light now on faces wild with delirium, now on swollen unmoving bodies, perhaps already

121

dead. Nor was the horror all to the eyes; piercing cries and deep groans rose from this multitude into the sweating air in a unison to which the engines played ground-bass.

At length, in the furthest corner, he came to two men whose faces made him start; he bent to examine them more closely. The serenely joyful days of the long-ago voyage returned to his mind; Antonio and Sabrinus in all their luck-bringing radiance; and the fearful term of it, their flight, their plunge to death. But had they somehow swum to safety? Was it possible that they had after all been rescued? For here they lay—they or their doubles?

Long he looked—turned away—looked again. The features were the same; yet the faces looked darker. And the torn clothing on their thin bodies was of a kind traditional to one of the Malay Islands. Moreover the language in which, unconscious of him, they muttered in their fever, was not the Mediterranean tongue of Antonio and Sabrinus. But they lay, in their hammocks, so close to one another—a ring of difference invisibly separating them from the mass of men, as it had separated Antonio and Sabrinus. Could it be that, rescued unimaginably from the storm, they had landed together on some island and in amnesia, or from mysterious will to obliterate all that had been, made its language their own? What of their hatred? If they had lived, then, had it passed, had they resumed their calm affection?

Or were they without substance, were they images and shadows of himself?

He turned to see if others saw them, or if he had conjured them to his private sight. But there was no one to ask, for all were absorbed in their own agonies. Back to the darkened faces, changed and yet the same, he looked, and saw that they were dying. Each was speaking, long and low, neither seeming to hear the other. Whether they had objective life or were parts of himself, he knew the same spirit informed them that had lit and darkened the forms of Antonio and Sabrinus.

Next day they did indeed die and with others were buried

at sea. But—he told me—not only then but now at the mo-
ment of recounting—he felt they would return to him, or he
to them.

His inquiries clarified nothing—they were two among a
crowd of Lascar hands. He left the ship at her port of desti-
nation and stayed ashore for over a year, drifting from one
occupation to another; but at length returned to the sea. He
has not yet seen them again, Antonio and Sabrinus.

A darkness enclosed the whole story
though in the beginning
a serene, even, sourceless light
veiled the darkness.

Did they know one another?
The hammocks were slung
one alongside the other
but the two sailors each addressed darkness.

Was it Antonio and Sabrinus or his double shadow?
Were they his shadow and themselves?
Had their intensity a substance
out of his sight?

Darkness enclosed his story. He would be waiting
to see them again.

She, returned in the form of youth
black of hair and dress
curls deaf in a poem.

He, returned, sits as he would never sit
perched on a radiator, smoking,
balking sullenly at an obscure outrage.

Only she who still lives, not as then but in
the white hair of today, awkwardly
laughs, at a loss for right words.
Three familiar spirits present to me.

The lamb and the ram removed
from the packing case are neither
gentle nor potent, but gray dead
of having never lived, weightless
plaster forms. What comes

live (though a toy) out of the box
is a black fox. Is it a fox?

The dead girl rejoices (But wait—
only now I remember she too is living
changed by time and inward fires.)
She takes the black animal I give her
in her arms, its sharp nose
poked at the long poem she is sunk in.

He is gone to another room angry
because the boy-child has seen
a diagram of the womb. Why?
Implacably laughing

(now I laugh too) but unsure
of my justice, I turn to assuage
a quick fear my black sister is prying

into my world, but the garnered
poems, stirring letters, dreams,
are undisturbed on the open desk.
She reads on and is dear to me.

Xochipilli

Xochipilli, god of spring
                        is sitting
on the earth floor, gazing
into a fire. In the fire
a serpent is preening, uncoiling.

'From thy dung
the red flowers,' says the god.

By the hearth
bodies of hares and mice,
food for the snake.

'From thy bones
white flowers,' says the god.

Rain dances many-footed
on the thatch. Raindrops
leap into the fire, the serpent hisses.

'From this music
seeds of the grass
that shall sing when the wind blows.'
                        The god stirs the fire.

Between town and the
old house, an inn—
the Half-Way House.
So far one could ride, I remember,

the rest was an uphill walk,
a mountain lane with
steep banks and sweet
hedges, half walls of

gray rock. Looking
again at this looking-glass face
unaccountably changed in a week,
three weeks, a month,

I think without thinking of
Half-Way House. Is it
the thought that this far
I've driven at ease, as in a bus,

a country bus where one could talk to the driver?
Now on foot towards the village;
the dust clears, silence
draws in around one. I hear
the rustle and hum of the fields: alone.

It must be the sense
of essential solitude that chills me
looking into my eyes.
I should remember

the old house at the walk's ending,
a square place with a courtyard,

granaries, netted strawberry-beds,
a garden that was many

gardens, each one
a world hidden from the
next by leaves, enlaced trees,
fern-hairy walls, gilly-flowers.

I should see, making
a strange face at myself,
nothing to fear in the thought of
Half-Way House—

the place one got down
to walk—. What is
this shudder, this
dry mouth?

Think, please, of the quarry pool,
the garden's furthest
garden, of your childhood's
joy in its solitude.

The Park

A garden of illusions!
Hidden by country trees, elm, oak,
wise thorn, and the tall green hedges of a maze,
the carpenters are preparing marvels!

But across the street the family
only glance toward the park gates,

stand clustered,
hesitant in their porch.

Already a ghost of fire
glides on the lake! In a mist
the flames of its body
pass shuddering over the dark ripples.

But they turn their heads
away, the tall people,
they talk and delay.

Waiting, I leap over
beds of glowing heart's-ease,
leaf-gold, fox-red, violet, deep
fur-brown, sailing high and slow

above them, descending
light and soft at their far borders.

But across the ice-crackling roadway
the house stands in midwinter daylight
and my friends neither in nor out of the house
still ignore the preparations of magic

the darkening of the garden
the flashes that may be summer lightning or
trials of illusion, the balconies
carved in a branchless towering oak.

Only the boy, my son, at last
ready, comes, and discovers joyfully
a man playing the horn
that is the true voice of the fire-ghost,

and believes in all wonders to come
in the park over-the-way,

country of open secrets where the elm
shelters the construction of gods
and true magic exceeds all design.

Art

(after Gautier)

The best work is made
from hard, strong materials,
     obstinately precise—
the line of the poem, onyx, steel.

It's not a question of
false constraints—but
     to move well and get somewhere
wear shoes that fit.

To hell with easy rhythms—
sloppy mules that anyone can
     kick off or
step into.

Sculptor, don't bother with modeling
pliant clay; don't let
     a touch of your thumb
set your vision while it's still vague.

Pit yourself against granite,
hew basalt, carve hard ebony—
     intractable
guardians of contour.

Renew the power men had in Azerbaijan
to cast ethereal intensity in bronze
    and give it
force to endure any number of thousand years.

Painter, let be the 'nervous scratches' the
trick spontaneity; learn to see again,
    construct, break through
to 'the thrill of continuance with the appearance of all its
      changes,'[1]

towards that point where 'art becomes
a realization with which the urge to live
    collaborates as a mason.'[2] Use
'the mind's tongue, that works and tastes into the very rock
      heart.'[3]

Our lives flower and pass. Only robust
works of the imagination live in eternity,
    Tlaloc, Apollo,
dug out alive from dead cities.

And the austere coin
a tractor turns up in a
    building site
reveals an emperor.

The gods die every day
but sovereign poems go on breathing
    in a counter-rhythm that mocks
the frenzy of weapons, their impudent power.

Incise, invent, file to poignance;

[1] *Cezanne*
[2] *Jean Hélion*
[3] *Ruskin*

130

make your elusive dream
      seal itself
in the resistant mass of crude substance.

To the Snake

Green Snake, when I hung you round my neck
and stroked your cold, pulsing throat
      as you hissed to me, glinting
arrowy gold scales, and I felt
      the weight of you on my shoulders,
and the whispering silver of your dryness
      sounded close at my ears—

Green Snake—I swore to my companions that certainly
      you were harmless! But truly
I had no certainty, and no hope, only desiring
      to hold you, for that joy,
                    which left
a long wake of pleasure, as the leaves moved
and you faded into the pattern
of grass and shadows, and I returned
smiling and haunted, to a dark morning.

INDEX OF TITLES

132

133